The Complaint of Peace

The
Complaint of Peace

Translated from the
Querela Pacis (A.D. 1521)

Desiderius Erasmus

Open  Court
La Salle, Illinois

Publisher's Note
This 1974 Open Court Paperback is an unabridged
reproduction of the original 1917 Open Court
clothbound edition, which in turn was reprinted from a
rare old English version. It is probably the 1802 reprint
of the translation made by T. Paynell but published
anonymously.

ISBN: 0-87548-195-7

The Complaint of Peace

THE COMPLAINT OF PEACE.

(Peace speaks in her own person.)

THOUGH I certainly deserve no ill treatment
from mortals, yet if the insults and repulses
I receive were attended with any advantage to
them, I would content myself with lamenting in
silence my own unmerited indignities and man's
injustice. But since, in driving me away from them,
they remove the source of all human blessings,
and let in a deluge of calamities on themselves,
I am more inclined to bewail their misfortune,
than complain of ill usage to myself; and I am
reduced to the necessity of weeping over and com-
miserating those whom I wished to view rather as
objects of indignation than of pity.

For though rudely to reject one who loves them
as I do, may appear to be savage cruelty; to feel
an aversion for one who has deserved so well of
them, base ingratitude; to trample on one who
has nursed and fostered them with all a parent's
care, an unnatural want of filial affection; yet vol-
untarily to renounce so many and so great advantages as I always bring in my train, to go in quest

of evils infinite in number and shocking in nature,
how can I account for such perverse conduct, but
by attributing it to downright madness? We may
be angry with the wicked, but we can only pity
the insane. What can I do but weep over them?
And I weep over them the more bitterly, because
they weep not for themselves. No part of their
misfortune is more deplorable than their insensi-
bility to it. It is one great step to convalescence
to know the extent and inveteracy of a disease.

Now, if I, whose name is Peace, am a personage
glorified by the united praise of God and man, as
the fountain, the parent, the nurse, the patroness,
the guardian of every blessing which either heaven
or earth can bestow; if without me nothing is
flourishing, nothing safe, nothing pure or holy,
nothing pleasant to mortals, or grateful to the
Supreme Being; if, on the contrary, war is one
vast ocean, rushing on mankind, of all the united
plagues and pestilences in nature; if, at its deadly
approach, every blossom of happiness is instantly
blasted, every thing that was improving gradually
degenerates and dwindles away to nothing, every
thing that was firmly supported totters on its
foundation, every thing that was formed for long
duration comes to a speedy end, and every thing
that was sweet by nature is turned into bitterness;
if war is so unhallowed that it becomes the deadliest bane of piety and religion; if there is nothing
more calamitous to mortals, and more detestable
to heaven, I ask, how in the name of God, can I
believe those beings to be rational creatures; how
can I believe them to be otherwise than stark mad;
who, with such a waste of treasure, with so ardent

a zeal, with so great an effort, with so many arts, so much anxiety, and so much danger, endeavour to drive me away from them, and purchase endless misery and mischief at a price so high?

If they were wild beasts who thus despised and rejected me, I could bear it more patiently; because I should impute the affront to nature, who had implanted in them so savage a disposition. If I were an object of hatred to dumb creatures, I could overlook their ignorance, because the powers of mind necessary to perceive my excellence have been denied to them. But it is a circumstance equally shameful and marvellous, that though nature has formed one animal, and one alone, with powers of reason, and a mind participating of divinity; one animal, and one alone, capable of sentimental affection and social union; I can find admission among the wildest of wild beasts, and the most brutal of brutes, sooner than with this one animal; the rational, immortal animal called man.

Among the celestial bodies that are revolving over our heads, though the motions are not the same, and though the force is not equal, yet they move, and ever have moved, without clashing, and in perfect harmony. The very elements themselves, though repugnant in their nature, yet, by a happy equilibrium, preserve eternal peace; and amid the discordancy of their constituent principles, cherish, by a friendly intercourse and coalition, an uninterrupted concord.

In living bodies, how all the various limbs harmonize, and mutually combine, for common defence against injury! What can be more heterogeneous, and unlike, than the body and the soul? and yet with what strong bonds nature has united them, is evident from the pang of separation. As life itself is nothing else but the concordant union of body and soul, so is health the harmonious co-operation of all the parts and functions of the body.

Animals destitute of reason live with their own kind in a state of social amity. Elephants herd together; sheep and swine feed in flocks; cranes and crows take their flight in troops; storks have their public meetings to consult previously to their emigration, and feed their parents when unable to feed themselves; dolphins defend each other by mutual assistance; and everybody knows, that both ants and bees have respectively established by general agreement, a little friendly community.

But I need dwell no longer on animals, which, though they want reason, are evidently furnished with sense. In trees and plants one may trace the vestiges of amity and love. Many of them are barren, unless the male plant is placed on their vicinity. The vine embraces the elm, and other plants cling to the vine. So that things which have no powers of sense to perceive any thing else, seem strongly to feel the advantages of union.

But plants, though they have not powers of perception, yet, as they have life, certainly approach very nearly to those things which are endowed with sentient faculties. What then is so completely insensible as stony substance? yet even in this, there appears to be a desire of union. Thus the loadstone attracts iron to it, and holds it fast in its embrace, when so attracted. Indeed, the attraction of cohesion, as a law of love, takes place throughout all inanimate nature.

I need not repeat, that the most savage of the savage tribes in the forest, live among each other in amity. Lions show no fierceness to the lion race. The boar does not brandish his deadly tooth against his brother boar. The lynx lives in peace with the lynx. The serpent shews no venom in his intercourse with his fellow serpent; and the loving kindness of wolf to wolf is proverbial.

But I will add a circumstance still more marvellous. The accursed spirits, by whom the concord between heaven and human beings was originally interrupted, and to this day continues interrupted, hold union with one another, and preserve their usurped power, such as it is, by unanimity![1]

Yet man to man, whom, of all created beings, concord would most become, and who stands most in need of it, neither nature, so powerful and irresistible in every thing else, can reconcile; neither human compacts unite; neither the great advantages which would evidently arise from unanimity combine, nor the actual feeling and experience of the dreadful evils of discord cordially endear. To all men the human form is the same, the sound made by the organs of utterance similar; and while other species of animals differ from each other chiefly in the shape of their bodies, to men alone is given a reasoning power, which is indeed common to all men, yet in a manner so exclusive, that it is not at the same time common

[1] Thus Milton:
    "O shame to men! Devil with devil damned
    Firm concord holds; men only disagree."

to any other living creature. To this distinguished being is also given the power of speech, the most conciliating instrument of social connection and cordial love. Throughout the whole race of men are sown by nature the seeds of virtue, and of every excellent quality. From nature man receives a mild and gentle disposition, so prone to reciprocal benevolence that he delights to be loved for the pleasure of being loved, without any view to interest; and feels a satisfaction in doing good, without a wish or prospect of remuneration. This disposition to do disinterested good, is natural to man, unless in a few instances, where, corrupted by depraved desires, which operate like the drugs of Circe's cup, the human being has degenerated to the brute. Hence even the common people, in the ordinary language of daily conversation, denominate whatever is connected with mutual good will, humane; so that the word humanity no longer describes man's nature, merely in a physical sense; but signifies humane manners, or a behaviour, worthy the nature of man, acting his proper part in civil society.

Tears also are a distinctive mark fixed by nature, and appropriated to her favourite, man. They are a proof of placability, a forgiving temper; so that if any trifling offence be given or taken, if a little cloud of ill humour darken the sunshine, there soon falls a gentle shower of tears, and the cloud melts into a sweet serenity.

Thus it appears, in what various ways nature has taught man her first great lesson of love and union. Nor was she content to allure the benevolence by the pleasurable sensations attending it;

nor did she think she has done enough, when she rendered friendship pleasant; and therefore she determined to make it necessary. For this purpose, she so distributed among various men different endowments of the mind and the body, that no individual should be so completely furnished with all of them, but that he should want the occasional assistance of the lowest orders, and even of those who are most moderately furnished with ability. Nor did she give the same talents either in kind or in degree to all, evidently meaning that the inequality of her gifts should be ultimately equalized by a reciprocal interchange of good offices and mutual assistance. Thus, in different countries, she has caused different commodities to be produced, that expediency itself might introduce commercial intercourse.

She furnished other animals with appropriate arms or weapons for defence or offence, but man alone she produced unarmed, and in a state of perfect imbecillity, that he might find his safety in association and alliance with his fellow-creatures. It was necessity which led to the formation of communities; it was necessity which led communities to league with each other, that, by the union of their force, they might repel the incursion either of wild beasts or banditti. So that there is nothing in the whole circle of human affairs, which is entirely sufficient of itself for self-maintenance, or self-defence.

In the very commencement of life, the human race had been extinct, unless conjugal union had continued the race. With difficulty could man be born into the world, or as soon as born would

he die, leaving life at the very threshold of existence, unless the friendly hand of the careful ma-
tron, and the affectionate assiduities of the nurse,
lent their aid to the helpless babe. To preserve
the poor infant, Nature has given the fond mother
the tenderest attachment to it, so that she loves it
even before she sees it.

Nature, on the other hand, has given the children a strong affection for the parent, that they
may become supports, in their turn, to the imbecillity of declining age; and that thus filial piety
may remunerate (after the manner of the stork)
to the second childhood of decrepitude, the tender cares experienced in infancy from parental
love. Nature has also rendered the bonds both of
kindred and affinity strong; a similarity of natural
disposition, inclinations, studies, nay of external
form, becomes a very powerful cause of attachment; and there is a secret sympathy of minds,
a wonderful lure to mutual affection, which the
ancients, unable to account for, attributed, in their
admiration of it, to the tutelar genius, or the
guardian angel.

By such and so many plain indications of her
meaning has Nature taught mankind to seek peace,
and ensure it. She invites them to it by various
allurements, she draws them to it by gentle violence, she compels them to it by the strong arm
of necessity. After all, then, what infernal being,
all-powerful in mischief, bursting every bond of
nature asunder, fills the human bosom with an insatiable rage for war? If familiarity with the
sight had not first destroyed all surprise at it, and
custom, soon afterwards, blunted the sense of its

evil, who could be prevailed upon to believe that those wretched beings are possessed of rational souls, the intellects and feelings of human creatures, who contend, with all the rage of furies, in everlasting feuds, and litigations, ending in murder! Robbery, blood, butchery, desolation, confound, without distinction, every thing sacred and profane. The most hallowed treaties, mutually confirmed by the strongest sanctions, cannot stop the enraged parties from rushing on to mutual destruction, whenever passion or mistaken interest urges them to the irrational decision of the battle.

Though there were no other motive to preserve peace, one would imagine that the common name of man might be sufficient to secure concord between all who claim it. But be it granted that Nature has no effect on men as men, (though we have seen that Nature rules as she ought to do in the brute creation), yet, must not Christ therefore avail with christians? Be it granted that the suggestions of nature have no effect with a rational being, (though we see them have great weight even on inanimate things without sense) yet, as the suggestions of the christian religion are far more excellent than those of nature, why does not the christian religion persuade those who profess it, of a truth which it recommends above all others, that is, the expediency and necessity of *peace on earth*, and *good-will towards men;* or at least, why does it fail of effectually dissuading from the unnatural, and more than brutal, madness of waging war?

When I, whose name is Peace, do but hear the

word Man pronounced, I eagerly run to him as to a being created purposely for me, and confidently promising myself, that with him I may live for ever in uninterrupted tranquillity; but when I also hear the title of Christian added to the name of Man, I fly with additional speed, hoping that with christians I may build an adamantine throne, and establish an everlasting empire.

But here also, with shame and sorrow, I am compelled to declare the result. Among Christians, the courts of justice, the palaces of princes, the senate-houses, and the churches, resound with the voice of strife, more loudly than was ever heard among nations who knew not Christ. Insomuch that though the multitude of wrangling advocates always constituted a great part of the world's misfortune, yet even this number is nothing compared with the successive inundation of suitors always at law.

I behold a city enclosed with walls. Hope springs in my bosom that men, christian men, must live in concord here, if any where, surrounded, as they are, by the same ramparts, governed by the same laws, embarked, as it were, in the same bottom, in the voyage of life, and therefore exposed to one common danger. But, ill-fated as I am, here also I find all happiness vitiated by dissension, that I can scarcely discover a single tenement in which I can take up my residence for the space of a few days only, unmolested.

But I leave the common people, who are tossed about, like the waves, by the winds of passion. I enter the courts of kings as into a harbour, from the storm of folly. Here, say I to myself, here must be a place for Peace to lodge in. These personages are wiser than the vulgar; they are the minds of the commonalty, the eyes of the people. They claim also to be the vicegerents of Him who was the teacher of charity, the Prince of Peace, from whom I come with letters of recommendation, addressed, indeed, in general, to all men, but more particularly to such as these.

Appearances, on my entrance into the palace, promise well. I see men saluting each other with the blandest, softest, gentlest expressions of respect and love; I see them shaking hands, and embracing with the most ardent professions of esteem; I see them dining together, and enjoying convivial pleasures in high glee and jollity; I see every outward sign of the kindest offices and humanity; but sorry am I to add, that I do not see the least symptom of sincere friendship. It is all paint and varnish. Every thing is corrupted by open faction, or by secret grudges and animosities. In one word, so far am I from finding in the palaces of princes a habitation for Peace, that in them I discover all the embryos, seminal principles, and sources of all the wars that ever cursed mankind, and desolated the universe.

Unfortunate as I am in my researches for a place to rest in, whither shall I next repair? I failed among kings, it is true; but perhaps the epithet great belongs to kings, rather than good, wise, or learned; and perhaps they are more under the influence of caprice and passion than of sound and sober discretion. I will repair to the learned world. It is said, learning makes the man; philosophy, something more than man; and theology exalts man to the divine nature. Harassed as I am with the research, I shall surely find among these a safe retreat to rest my head in undisturbed repose. Here also I find war of another kind, less bloody indeed, but not less furious. Scholar wages war with scholar; and, as if truth could be changed by change of place, some opinions must never pass over the sea, some never can surmount the Alps, and others do not even cross the Rhine; nay, in the same university, the rhetorician is at variance with the logician, and the theologist with the lawyer. In the same kind of profession, the scotist contends with the thomist, the nominalist with the realist, the platonic with the peripatetic; insomuch that they agree not in the minutest points, and often are at daggers drawing *de lana caprina,* till the warmth of disputation advances from argument to abusive language, and from abusive language to fisty-cuffs; and, if they do not proceed to use real swords and spears, they stab one another with pens dipt in the venom of malice; they tear one another with biting libels,. and dart the deadly arrows of their tongues against their opponent's reputation.

So often disappointed, whither shall I repair? Whither, but to the houses of religion? Religion! that anchor in the storm of life? The profession of religion is indeed common to all christians; but they who come recommended to us under the appellation of priests, profess it in a more peculiar manner, by the name they bear, the service they perform, and the ceremonies they observe.

When I take a view of them at a distance, every outward and visible sign makes me conclude, that among them, at least, I shall certainly find a safe asylum. I like the looks of their white surplices; for white is my own favourite colour. I see figures of the cross about them, all symbolical of peace. I hear them all calling one another by the pleasant name of brother, a mark of extraordinary goodwill and charity; I hear them salute each other with the words, "Peace be unto you": apparently happy in an address so ominous of joy. I see a community of all things; I see them incorporated in a regular society, with the same place of worship, the same rules, and the same daily congregation. Who can avoid being confidently certain that here, if no where else in the world, a habitation will be found for peace?

O, shame to tell! there is scarcely one man in these religious societies that is on good terms with his own bishop; though even this might be passed over as a trifling matter, if they were not torn to pieces by party disputes among each other. Where is the priest to be found, who has not a dispute with some other priest? Paul thinks it an insufferable enormity that a christian should go to law with a christian; and shall a priest contend with a priest, a bishop with a bishop? But perhaps it may be offered as an apology for these men, that, by long intercourse with men of the world, and by possessing such things as the world chiefly values, they have gradually adopted the manners of the world, even in the retreat of the church and the cloister. To themselves I leave them to strive about that property, which they claim by prescription.

There remains one order of the clergy, who are so tied to religion by vows that, if they were inclined, they could no more shake it off, than the tortoise can get rid of the shell which he carries on his back, like a house. I should hope, if I had not been so often disappointed, that, among these persons, coming in the name of peace, I should gain a welcome reception. However, that I may leave no stone unturned, I go and try whether I may be allowed to fix my residence here. Do you wish to know the result of the experiment? I never received a ruder repulse. What indeed could I expect, where religion herself seems to be at war with religion. There are just as many parties as there are fraternities. The dominicans disagree with the minorites, the benedictines with the bernardines; so many modes of worship, so various the rites and ceremonies; they cannot agree in any particular; every one likes his own, and therefore damns all others. Nay, the same fraternity is rent into parties; the observantes inveigh against the coletae; both unite in their hatred of a third sort, which, though it derives its name from a convent, yet, in no article, can come to an amicable convention.

By this time, as you may imagine, despairing of almost every place, I formed a wish that I might be permitted to seek a quiet retreat in the obscurity of some little inconsiderable monastery. With reluctance I must declare, what I wish were untrue, that I have not yet been able to find one which is not corrupted and spoiled by intestine jars and animosities. I blush to relate on what childish, flimsy causes, old men, venerable for their grey beards and their gowns, and in their own opinions not only deeply learned, but holy, involve themselves in endless strife.

I now cherished a pleasing hope that I might find a place in private, domestic life, amid the apparent happiness of conjugal and family endearment. It was surely reasonable to expect it from such promising circumstances, as an equal partnership founded on the choice of the heart, in the same house, the same fortune, the same bed, the same progeny; add to this, the mysterious union by which two become virtually one. But here also Eris, the goddess of discord, had insinuated herself, and had torn asunder the strongest bands of conjugal attachment, by disagreement in temper; and yet, in the domestic circle, I could much sooner have found a place than among the professed religious, notwithstanding their fine titles, their splendid dresses, images, crucifixes, and their various ceremonies, all which hold out the idea of perfect charity, the very bonds of peace.

At length I felt a wish that I might find a snug and secure dwelling-place in the bosom, at least, of some one man. But here also I failed. One and the same man is at war with himself. Reason wages war with the passions; one passion with another passion. Duty calls one way, and inclination another. Lust, anger, avarice, ambition, are all up in arms, each pursuing its own purposes, and warmly engaged in the battle.

Such then and so fierce, ought not men to blush at the appellation of christians, differing, as they do essentially, from the peculiar and distinguishing excellence of Christ? Consider the whole of his life; what is it, but one lesson of concord and mutual love? What do his precepts, what do his parables inculcate, but peace and charity? Did that excellent prophet Isaiah, when he foretold the coming of Christ as an universal reconciler, represent him as an earthly lord, a satrap, a grandee, or courtier? Did he announce him as a mighty conqueror, a burner of villages, a destroyer of towns, as one who was to triumph over the slaughter and misery of wretched mortals? No. How then did he announce him? As the Prince of Peace. The prophet, intending to describe him as the most excellent of all the princes that ever came into the world, drew the title of that superior excellence, from what is itself the most excellent of all things, Peace. Nor is it to be wondered, that Isaiah, an inspired prophet, viewed Peace in this light, when Silius Italicus, a heathen poet, has written my character in these words:

> ....Pax optima rerum
> Quas homini natura dedit..........
>
> No boon that nature ever gave to man,
> May be compared with peace.

The mystic minstrel, the sweet psalmist, has also sung:

"In Salem (a place of peace) is his tabernacle." Not in tents, not in camps, did this prince, mighty to save, fix his residence; but in Salem, the city of peace. He is, indeed, the Prince of Peace; peace is his dear delight, and war his abomination.

Again, the prophet Isaiah calls the work of righteousness, peace; meaning the same thing with Paul, (who was himself converted from the turbulent Saul, to a preacher of peace) when preferring charity to all other gifts of the secret spirit of God, he thundered in the ears of the Corinthians my eulogium, with an eloquence which arose from the fine feelings of his bosom, animated by grace, and warm with benevolence. Why may I not glory in having been celebrated by one so celebrated himself, as this great apostle? In another place he calls Christ the God of Peace; and in a third, the Peace of God; plainly indicating, that these two characters so naturally coalesce, that Peace cannot come where God is not; and that where Peace is not, God cannot come.

In the sacred volumes we find the holy ministers of God called messengers of peace; from which it is obvious to conclude, whose ministers those men must be, who are the messengers of war. Hear this, ye mighty warriors and mark under whose banners ye fight;—they are those of that accursed being who first sowed strife between man and his maker. To this first fatal strife are to be ascribed all the woes that mortal man is doomed to feel.

It is frivolous to argue, as some do, that God is called, in the mysterious volumes, the God of hosts, and the God of vengeance. There is a great difference between the God of the Jews and the God of the Christians, notwithstanding God, in his own essence, is one and the same. But if we must still retain the ancient jewish titles of God, let God be called the God of hosts, while, by the word hosts, is understood, the phalanx of divine

graces, by whose energy good men are enabled to
route and destroy the vices, those deadliest enemies
of human felicity.   Let him still be styled God of
vengeance, provided you understand it to be vengeance on those sins which rob us of repose.   In
like manner, the examples of bloody slaughter
with which the jewish histories are stuffed, should
be used, not as incentives to the butchery of our
fellow-creatures, but to the utter extermination
of all bad passions, hostile to our virtue and happiness, from the territory of our own bosoms.

To proceed, however, as I had begun, with
scriptural passages in favour of peace.   Whenever they mean to describe perfect happiness,
they always denote it by the name of peace; as
Isaiah, "My people shall repose in the beauty of
peace"; so also, "Peace upon Israel."   Again,
Isaiah expresses a rapturous admiration of them
who bring glad tidings of peace.   Whoever of the
sacred writers announces Christ, announces peace
on earth.   Whoever proclaims war, proclaims him
who is as unlike Christ as it is possible to be—
the grand destroyer.

What induced the Son of God to come down
from heaven to earth, but a gracious desire to
reconcile the world to his Father? to cement the
hearts of men by mutual and indissoluble love?
and lastly, to reconcile man to himself and bid
him be at peace with his own bosom?   For my
sake, then, he was sent on this gracious embassy;
it was my business which he condescended to
transact; and therefore he appointed Solomon to
be a type of himself; the very name Solomon signifying a peace-maker.   Great and illustrious as

King David is represented; yet, because he was a king who delighted in war, and because he was polluted with human gore, he was not permitted to build the house of the Lord, he was not worthy to be made the type of Christ.

Now then, warrior, halt and consider; if wars, undertaken and carried on at the command of the Deity, (as was the case in David's wars) pollute and render a man unholy, what will be the effect of wars of ambition, wars of revenge, and wars of furious anger? If the blood of heathens defiled the pious king who shed it, what will be the effect on christian kings, of so copious an effusion of the blood of christians, caused solely by royal revenge?

I do beseech your christian majesty, (if you are a christian in any thing besides your title) to contemplate the model of him who is your sovereign; observe how he entered upon his reign, how he conducted it, how he departed from this world, and learn to reign from his example. You will find that the very first object of your heart should be, to preserve your country in a state of peace.

At the nativity of Christ did the angels sound the clarion of war? The horrid din might have been addressed to the ears of Jews, for they were allowed to wage war. Such auspices were well enough adapted to those who thought it lawful to hate their enemies; but to the pacific race of future christians, the angels of peace sounded a far different note. Did they blow the shrill trumpet? Did they promise triumphs and trophies of victory? Far from it. What then did they announce? Peace and good will, in conformity with

the predictions of the prophets; and they announced them not to those who breathe war and
bloodshed, who delight in the instruments of destruction, but to those whose hearts are inclined
to concord.

Let me cover their malice with what cloke they
please; it is certain, that if they did not delight
in war, they would not be constantly engaged in
its conflicts.

But as for Christ, what else did he teach and
inculcate, but peace? He addressed those whom
he loved, with the auspicious words of peace:
Peace be with you, he repeatedly says; and prescribes this form of salutation, as alone worthy
of the christian character. And the apostles, duly
mindful of his precept and example, preface their
epistles with a wish for peace to those whom they
love. He who wishes health to his friend, wishes
a most desirable blessing; but he who wishes him
peace, wishes him the summit of human felicity.

As Christ had recommended peace during the
whole of his life, mark with what anxiety he en-
forces it at the approach of his dissolution. Love
one another, says he; as I have loved you, so love
one another; and again, my peace I give unto you,
my peace I leave you. Do you observe the legacy
he leaves to those whom he loves? Is it a pompous
retinue, a large estate, or empire? Nothing of
this kind. What is it then? peace he giveth, his
peace he leaveth; peace, not only with our near
connexions, but with enemies and strangers!

I wish you to consider with me, what it was
which he besought of his Father in his last prayer,
at the last supper, when death was at hand. It was

a remarkable prayer for one who knew that he should obtain whatever he requested. Father, says he, keep them in thy name, that they may be one, like as we are! Observe, I beseech you, what a wonderful union Christ requires in his followers; he does not pray that they may be of one mind, but that they may be one; nor does he mention this union in a vague manner, but says, "That they may be one, as we are," who are one and the same in a most perfect, yet unspeakable and inexplicable manner. He indicates at the same time, that mortals can obtain salvation, or immortality, by no other means than the preservation of peace among themselves, during the whole of this transitory life.

Moreover, as the kings of this world usually distinguish their subjects by some mark by which they may be known from others, especially in war, Christ has distinguished his subjects by the badge of mutual charity. By this, says he, shall all men know that you are my disciples; not if you wear this or that uniform, not if you eat this or that kind of food, not if you fast on this or that occasion, not if you say such or such a portion of the psalms; but if you love one another, and that not in the common way, but, as I have loved you. The precepts of philosophers are innumerable, the laws of Moses are various, as well as the edicts of princes; but one commandment, says he, I give you, and it is, love one another.

When he prescribed a form of prayer to his disciples, did he not admonish us, in a wonderful manner, in the very beginning of it, concerning the unanimity which christians are bound to pre-

serve? Our Father! says he. It is the prayer of
one; yet it is the common request of all. All then
are one house, one family, depending upon one
Father; and how can it possibly be allowed that,
in such circumstances, they should be tearing each
other to pieces in never-ceasing wars?

How can you say our Father, addressing the
universal parent, while you are thrusting the sharp
steel into the bowels of your brother? for such
you confess him to be by this very prayer, "Our
Father."

As Christ wished the sentiments of philan-
thropy, or universal concord, to be fixed deeply
in the hearts of all his followers, by what a variety
of emblems, parables, and precepts, has he incul-
cated the love of peace! He calls himself a shepherd, and his followers his sheep. And, let me
ask, did you ever see sheep fighting in earnest
with their fellow sheep, so as either to injure
limbs, or destroy life? or, what greater harm can
the wolves do, if the flock thus tear each other in
pieces?

When Christ calls himself the vine, and his
disciples the branches, what else did he mean to
express, but the most perfect union between him
and them, and between themselves? It would be
a prodigy, indeed, if a branch were to contend
with a branch of the same tree; and, is it less a
prodigy, that a christian fights with a christian?

If there be anything sacred to christians, surely
that ought to be deemed singularly sacred, and to
sink deeply into their hearts, which Christ delivered to them in his last dying commands; when
he was, as it were, making his will and testament,

and recommending to his sons those things which he wished might never fall into oblivion. And what is it which, on this solemn occasion, he teaches, commands, prescribes, entreats; but that they should preserve inviolate, mutual good-will, or charity? And what means the communion of the holy bread and wine, but a renewed sanction of indissoluble amity? As Christ knew that Peace could not be preserved, where men were struggling for office, for glory, for riches, for revenge, he roots out from the hearts of his disciples all passions which lead to these things; he forbids them absolutely and without exception, to resist evil; he commands them to do good to those who use them ill, and to pray for those who curse them. And, after this, shall kings presume to think themselves christians, who, on the slightest injury embroil the world in war?

He commands that the man who would be the chief among the people, should be their servant; nor endeavour to outdo others in any thing else but in being better than they, and in doing more good to his fellow-mortals. Then are not certain persons claiming to be chiefs, ashamed, for the sake of making some paltry addition to the outskirts of their domains, (already too large) to set the world in a flame?

He teaches you to live after the manner of the birds of the air, and the lilies of the field; trusting to Providence. He forbids your solicitude to extend to the morrow. He wishes you to depend entirely on God. He excludes all rich men, who trust in riches, from the kingdom of heaven. And yet are there crowned miscreants, who, for the

sake of a poor pittance of money, perhaps, after
all, not due to them, will not hesitate to spill
torrents of human blood in the field of battle?
Indeed, in these very times, the recovery of a sum
of money appears to be a very good cause of a
just and necessary war!

Christ seems to have had in view this tendency
in men to contend for trifles, when he bids his disciples to learn of him to be meek and lowly, and
to lay aside all dispositions to revenge. When he
orders them to leave their gift at the altar, nor
to offer it before they are reconciled to their
brother, does he not plainly insinuate, that unanimity is to be preferred to any thing else; and
that no oblation on the altar is acceptable to God,
unless it is presented by me? God refused the
Jewish offering, a goat perhaps, or a sheep, because it was offered by those who were at variance
with each other; and shall christians, at the very
time they are endeavouring to cut each other's
throats in the field of battle, dare to make an oblation at the holy communion of the Lord's supper? When he condescended to compare himself
to a hen gathering her chickens under her wing,
what a beautiful and expressive picture did he
delineate of christian unity? He gathers his
chickens under his wing; and shall christians, his
professed followers, dare to act the part of hawks
or kites?

Of a similar tendency is the comparison of himself to a cornerstone, at once supporting and uni-
ting the two walls which rest upon it; and how
then can it be reconcilable to the profession of
christians, that those who call themselves his

vicars or vicegerents, should excite the whole
world to arms, and set kingdom against kingdom?
They profess, as kings of christian countries, that
he is their great sovereign and reconciler; and yet
they cannot be reconciled to each other by any
arguments drawn from christianity. He reconciled
Pilate and Herod; and yet his own followers will
not be reconciled by his intervention. He chides
Peter, though half a Jew, who drew a sword in
his defence when his life was in immediate danger,
and orders him to put it up into its scabbard; and
yet christians keep the sword constantly drawn,
and are ever ready to use it on their brother
christians, on the most trifling provocation. Could
he wish himself, or his cause to be defended by a
sword, who, with his dying breath, prayed for his
murderers?

Every page of the christian scriptures, whether
you read those parts of the Old Testament which
have a reference to christianity, or the New, speaks
of little else but peace and concord; and yet the
whole life of the greater portion of christians is
employed in nothing so much as the concerns of
war. It is really more than brutal ferocity which
can neither be broken in, nor mitigated in its violence, by so many concurrent circumstances. It
were best to lay aside the name of christian at
once; or else to give proof of the doctrine of
Christ, by its only criterion, brotherly love. How
long shall your lives contradict your profession
and appellation? You may mark your houses,
your vestments, and your churches, with the cross,
as much as you please; but Christ will recognize

no other badge, than that which he himself prescribed, love of one another.

Men gathered together formerly for the purposes of devotion, saw him ascending into heaven; they that are now gathered together for the same purpose, are ordered to expect the descent of the Holy Ghost: he has promised to be always with those that are for such purposes gathered together; so that none can ever reasonably think to find him in the field of battle. With respect to the spirit of fire that descended on the apostles, what is it but charity? Nothing is more common property than fire. Without any loss, fire is lighted by fire. Would you be convinced that this spirit is the parent of concord? Mark the result of it. There was, says he, among them one heart and one soul. Withdraw the breath or spirit from the body, and immediately the fine contexture of its parts is totally destroyed. In like manner, withdraw peace, and the whole mysterious union with heaven, which forms the divine life, is at once dissolved. Divines tell us, that the heavenly spirit is infused into our hearts by the sacrament. If they tell us true, where is that peculiar effect of this spirit in those who take the sacrament, the one heart and the one soul? But if they tell us only an amusing story, why is such honour paid to useless things? So much I have ventured to say, not for the sake of detracting from the sanctity of the sacrament, but that christians may blush to find their manners correspond so little with their solemn profession.

What is meant by denominating the whole body of christian people, the church, but that it should admonish them that they are united, and ought therefore to be unanimous? Now, what possible agreement can there be between camps and a church? A church implies union and association; camps, disunion and discord. If you say you belong to the church, what can you have to do with the operations of war? If you say you do not belong to the church what have you to do with Christ?

But if you are all of the same house; if you all acknowledge the same head and master of the family; if you all militate under the same captain; if you all receive the same largesses, and are maintained by the same pay; if you are all in pursuit of the same great prize, why these tumults and disorders in your march? You see among those unnatural and cruel comrades, who advance in troops to perform the work of human butchery for hire, perfect concord maintained, because they are led on under the same standards; and shall not so many pacific circumstances unite the hearts of those whose bloodless warfare is to promote piety and peace? Do so many sacraments avail nothing in producing unanimity?

Baptism is common to you all; by means of this you are born again to Christ; you are cutt off from the world, and become ingrafted members of the body of Christ. Now what can conduce so much to unity and identity, as to be made members of one and the same body? From this incorporation with Christ, the petty distinctions of bond and free, greek and barbarian, male and female, cease to separate mankind; and all are one in Christ, who brings them all, whatever their local and

physical diversities may be, to unity and identity
of heart and disposition.

Among the scythians, they have a ceremony of
drinking a drop of each other's blood out of a
cup, as a cement of friendship; after which, those
who have partaken of it will hesitate at no hard-
ship in the service of each other, and will meet
death itself with alacrity, in mutual defence.
Shall heathens then deem that concord inviolable,
which a participation of a draught at the same
table has sanctioned; and shall not christians be
kept in love and charity by that heavenly bread,
and that mystic cup, which Christ himself ordained, in which they every day communicate,
constantly repeating, with the most solemn rites,
the holy feast of love? If Christ meant nothing
by this institution why is it kept up among christians to this day, with so many ceremonies? If
he meant the most serious and important benefit
to mankind, then why is it slightly regarded by
you, as if it were a farce, or a mere scenic exhibi-
tion? Does any man presume to go to that table,
the symbol of love; does any one presume to approach the feast of peace, who, at the same moment, meditates war against christians, and is pre-
paring to destroy those whom Christ died to save,
to spill the blood of those for whom Christ shed
his own!

Hearts unfeeling as the flint! In many partic-
ulars you are united by nature and necessity; yet
in life and action, where you may freely choose
your conduct, you are rent asunder by unaccount-
able dissension and strife! By the law of nature,

you are all born into the world, of a woman; by the law of necessity, you all wax old and feeble, and then sink into the grave. You are all sprung from the same first parent; you have all the same divine author of your religion; you are all redeemed by the same blood, initiated in the same holy rites, nourished in your spiritual growth by the same sacraments; and whatever advantage flows from all these combined, flows from the same fountain, and flows equally to all. You have all the same church, and all look for the same reward.

That heavenly Jerusalem, for which every true christian pants, derives its name from the beatific vision of peace, of which the church, in the mean time, is a typical representation. And how happens it, that the church itself differs so widely from its holy examples? Has nature availed nothing in her various instructions and lessons of love? Has Christ availed nothing, with all his mysteries, all his precepts, all his symbols of peace?

Adversity, or evil, if not good, will cause bad men to cling together; but neither adversity nor prosperity, neither good nor evil, will effect a perfect coalition among christians. Let us turn our attention to the adverse side, the evils of life, and see if they produce any effect in urging christians to unite for mutual comfort and protection.

What is more brittle than the life of man? Supposing it unbroken by casualties, how short its natural duration! How liable to disease; how exposed to momentary accidents! Yet, though the natural and inevitable evils are more and greater than can be borne with patience, man, fool as he is, brings the greatest and worst calamities

upon his own head. Though condemned to feel the
effects of his folly, yet so blind is he that he cannot see it. Headlong he goes with an impetuosity
so precipitate as to burst and tear asunder every
tie of nature, every bond of Christ. To arms he
rushes at all times and in all places; no bounds
to his fury, no end to his destructive vengeance.
Together they engage, nation with nation, city
with city, king with king; and to gratify the folly
or greedy ambition of two poor puny mortals,
who shortly shall die by nature, like insects of a
summer's day, all human affairs are disarranged,
and whirled in confusion. I will pass over the
sad tragedy of war, acted on the bloody stage of
the world in times long past.

Let us only take a retrospect of the last ten years.
In what part of the world, during that short space,
have there not been bloody battles both by sea
and land? What country in which the earth has
not been fertilized with the blood of christians
shed by christians? What river or sea that has not
been discoloured with purple tide of human gore?
Yes, I am ashamed to declare, that christians fight
more savagely than jews, than heathens, than the
beasts of the field? The warlike spirit which the
jews displayed towards aliens, christians are bound
to display against their vices; but, on the contrary,
they chuse to be at peace with their vices, and at
war with their fellow-creatures. And yet, as an
apology for the jews, it must be said, that they
were led to war, in a particular case, by divine
command, for the purpose of divine Providence;
while the christians (remove but the poor flimsy
veil of false pretexts, and judge according to real

truth) you will find hurried into the crooked path of ambition by anger, the very worst counsellor, and allured to shed blood by an insatiable avarice of gold. The jews waged war with foreign nations; while the christians are, with the Turks, at peace, and, with one another, at war!

As to the heathen despots, it is true, the thirst of glory goaded them to battle; but yet even they conquered fierce and barbarous nations to civilize them; insomuch, that it was often an advantage to be conquered, the conquerors endeavouring to render every service in their power to the people whom they had subdued. They took pains to render their victories as little bloody as possible, that the conqueror might be rewarded with a more honourable renown, and that the clemency of the victor might afford consolation to the vanquished. But I blush to record, upon how infamously frivolous causes the world has been rouzed to arms by christian kings. One of them has found, or forged, an obsolete musty parchment, on which he makes a claim to a neighbouring territory. As if it signified a straw to mankind, thus called upon to shed blood, who is the person, or what the family of the ruling prince, whoever he be, provided he governs in such a manner as to consult and promote public felicity.

Another alleges that some punctilio, in a treaty of a hundred articles, has been infringed or neglected. A third owes a neighbouring king a secret grudge, on a private account, because he has married some princess whom he intended to be his consort, or uttered some sarcasm that reflects upon his royal person and character.

And, what is the basest and most flagitious conduct of all, there are crowned heads, who, with the
mean cunning that ever characterizes the despot,
contrive (because they find their own power weak-
ened by the people's union, and strengthened by
their division) to excite war without any substantial reason for a rupture; merely to break the
national union at home, and pillage the oppressed
people with impunity. There are infernal agents
enough, who fatten on the plunder of the people,
and have little to do in state affairs during the
time of peace, who easily manage to bring about
the wished-for rupture, and embroil an unoffending people in a war with an unoffending neigh-
bour. Nothing but a fury of hell could instil such
venom into the bosom of a christian.

Cruelty of despotism like this, in the hearts
of kings pretending to christianity, was never
equalled by Dionysius, Mezentius, Phalaris, the
most infamous tyrants of antiquity! Degraded
wretches! Brutes, not men! Great only by the
abuse of greatness! Fools in every thing but the
art of doing mischief! unanimous in nothing but
in defrauding and oppressing the public! Yet,
wretches, brutes, and fools as they are, they are
called christians, and have the impudence to go
with a face of piety to church, and dare even to
kneel at the altar. Pests of mankind, worthy to
be transported out of civil society, and carried
with convicts to the remotest islands, in exile for
life.

If it be true that christians are members of one
body, how happens it that every christian does

not sympathize and rejoice in every other christian's welfare? Now, however, it seems to be
cause enough to commence a just and necessary
war, that a neighbouring land is in a more prosperous, flourishing, or free condition, than your
own. For, if you can but prevail upon yourselves
to speak the real truth, what, I ask, has excited,
and what continues at this very day to excite, so
many combined powers against the kingdom of
France, unless it be, that it is the finest and most
flourishing country in Europe? Nowhere is there
a more extensive territory; nowhere a more august
public council; nowhere greater unanimity, and,
on all these accounts united, nowhere greater
power....[1]

God made man unarmed. But anger and revenge have mended the work of God, and furnished his hands with weapons invented in hell.
Christians attack christians with engines of destruction, fabricated by the devil. A cannon! a
mortar! no human being could have devised them
originally; they must have been suggested by the
evil one. Nature, indeed, has armed lions with
teeth and claws, and bulls with horns; but who
ever saw them go in bodies to use their arms for
mutual destruction? What man ever saw so small
a number as even ten lions congregated to fight
ten bulls, and drawn up in battle array? But how
often have twenty thousand christians met an
equal number on the same plain, all prepared to
shoot each other, through the heart, or to plunge

[1] A few lines are here omitted, because, though descrip-
tive of France in the days of Erasmus, they now bear but
little resemblance to it.

the sword or bayonet through each other's bowels.
So little account do they make of hurting their
brethren, that they have not the smallest scruple
to spill every drop of blood in their bodies. Beasts
of the forest; your contests are at least excusable,
and sometimes amiable; ye fight only when driven
to madness by hunger, or to defend your young
ones; but as for those who call themselves your
lords, (men and christians) the faintest shadow
of an affront is sufficient to involve them in all the
horrors of premeditated war.

If the lower orders of the people were to act in
this manner, some apology might be found in their
supposed ignorance; if very young men were to
act in this manner, the inexperience of youth
might be pleaded in extenuation; if the poor laity
only were concerned, the frailty of the agents
might lessen the atrocity of the action: but the
very reverse of this is the truth. The seeds of
war are chiefly sown by those very people whose
wisdom and moderation, characteristic of their
rank and station, ought to compose and assuage
the impetuous passions of the people.

The people, the ignoble vulgar, despised as they
are, are the very persons who originally raise great
and fair cities to their proud eminence; who conduct the commercial business of them entirely;
and, by their excellent management, fill them with
opulence. Into these cities, after they are raised
and enriched by plebeians, creep the satraps and
grandees, like so many drones into a hive; pilfer
what was earned by others' industry; and thus,
what was accumulated by the labour of the many,

is dissipated by the profligacy of the few; what was built by plebeians on upright foundations, is leveled to the ground by cruelty and royal patrician injustice.

If the military transactions of old time are not worth remembrance, let him who can bear the loathsome employ, only call to mind the wars of the last twelve years; let him attentively consider the causes of them all, and he will find them all to have been undertaken for the sake of kings; all of them carried on with infinite detriment to the people; while, in most instances, the people had not the smallest conern either in their origin or their issue.

Then, as to young men being chiefly concerned in this mischief of exciting war; so far from it, that you hide your grey hairs with a helmet; *canitiem galea premitis*; and you deem it an honour to the hoary head of a christian, to encourage, or even take an active part in war, though the heathen poet, Ovid, says, *"turpe senex miles;"* that an old man, a warrior! is a loathsome object. Ovid's countrymen would have considered a fighting-man, or one that set others to fight, at seventy years old, a blood-thirsty dotard, with one foot in his grave, a monster of wickedness and folly.

As to the laity only being concerned, it is so far from true, that priests, whom God, under the severe and sanguinary dispensation of Moses, forbade to be polluted with blood, do not blush; that christian divines and preachers, the guides of our lives, do not blush; that professors of the purest divinity do not blush; that neither bishops, cardinals, nor Christ's own vicars, blush, to become the instigators, the very fire-brands of war, against which Christ, from whom they all pretend to derive the only authority they can have, expressed his utter detestation.

What possible consistency can there be between a mitre and a helmet, a pastoral staff and a sabre? between the volume of the gospel and a shield and buckler? How can it be consistent to salute the people with the words, "peace be with you," and, at the same time, to be exciting the whole world to bloody war! with the lips to speak peace, and with the hand, and every power of action, to be urging on havoc? Dare you describe Christ as a reconciler, a Prince of Peace, and yet palliate or commend war, with the same tongue; which in truth, is nothing less than to sound the trumpet before Christ and Satan at the same time? Do you presume, reverend sir, with your hood and surplice on, to stimulate the simple, inoffensive people to war, when they come to church, expecting to hear from your mouth the gospel of peace? Are you not apprehensive, lest what was said by those who announced the coming of Christ, "how beautiful are the feet of him that bringeth glad tidings of peace; who bringeth tidings of good, who bringeth tidings of salvation!" should be reversed, and addressed to you in this manner: "how foul is the tongue of priests; exhorting to war, inciting to evil, and urging men to destruction." Think of the incongruous idea, a bloody priest!

Among the old Romans, who retained something of true piety in the midst of heathenism, whoever entered on the office of pontifex maximus, or high priest, was obliged to swear that he would keep his hands unstained with blood; and that, if he were provoked, or even hurt by any aggressor, he would not avenge the injury. Titus Vespasian, a heathen emperor, kept the oath religiously, and is highly commended for it by a heathen writer. But among christians, as if shame had fled from earth, clergymen, solemnly consecrated to God, are often among the first to inflame the minds, both of king and people, to blood and devastation. They convert the sweet accents of the gospel to the trumpet of Mars; and, forgetting the dignity of their profession, run about making proselytes to their opinion, ready to do or suffer any thing, so long as they can but succeed in kindling the flames of war.

Kings who perhaps might otherwise have kept quiet, are set on fire by those very men, who ought, if they acted in character, to cool the ardour of warring potentates by their official and sacred authority. Nay, what is more monstrous still, clergymen actually wage war in person, and with a view to obtain shares in prizes or preferments; things, which the philosophers among the heathens held in contempt; and the contempt of which is the peculiar and appropriate distinction of men who profess to follow the apostles.

A very few years ago, when the world, labouring under a deadly fever, was running headlong to arms, the gospel trumpeters blew a blast from the pulpit, and inflamed the wretched kings of Europe to a paroxysm, running as they were fast enough of themselves into a state of downright insanity. Among the english, the clergy fulminated from the pulpit against the french; and among the

french, against the english. They all united in
instigating to war. Not one man among the clery
exhorted to peace; or, at least, not above one or
two, whose lives would perhaps be in danger, if I
were even now to name them.

The right reverend fathers in God, the holy
bishops, forgetting their personal and professional
dignity, were continually running to and fro, like
the evil-one, adding virulence to the public disease of the world, by their mischievous officious-
ness; instigating, on one hand, Julius the pope,
and, on the other, the surrounding kings, to push
on the war with vigour; as if both pope and kings
were not mad enough without their inflammatory
suggestions. In the mean time, the fathers in
God failed not to call their bloodthirsty rage, a
zeal for law, order, and religion.

To forward their sanguinary purposes, they
wrest the laws of heaven to a constructive meaning never meant, they misinterpret the writings
of good men, they misquote and misrepresent the
sacred scripture, I do not say, with the most bare-
faced impudence only, but the most blasphemous
impiety. Nay, matters are come to such a pass,
that it is deemed foolish and wicked to open one's
mouth against war, or to venture a syllable in
praise of peace; the constant theme of Christ's
eulogy. He is thought to be ill affected to the
king, and even to pay but little regard to the
people's interest, who recommends what is of all
things in the world the most salutary, to both
king and people, or dissuades from that which,
without any exception, is the most destructive.

In addition to all this, chaplains follow the army

to the field of battle; bishops preside in the camp, and, abandoning their churches, enlist in the service of Bellona. The war multiplies priests, bishops, and cardinals, among whom, to be a camp legate is deemed an honourable preferment, and worthy the successors of the apostles. It is therefore the less wonderful that priests should breathe the spirit of Mars, to whom Mars gives ecclesiastical rank, together with loaves and fishes.

It is a circumstance which renders the evil less capable of remedy, that the clergy cover over this most irreligious conduct with the cloke of religion. The colours in the regiments, (consecrated by ministers of peace!) bear the figure of the cross painted upon them. The unfeeling mercenary soldier, hired by a few pieces of paltry coin, to do the work of man-butcher, carries before him the standard of the cross; and that very figure becomes the symbol of war, which alone ought to teach every one that looks at it, that war ought to be utterly abolished. What hast thou to do with the cross of Christ on thy banners, thou blood-stained soldier? With such a disposition as thine; with deeds like thine, of robbery and murder, thy proper standard would be a dragon, a tiger, or a wolf!

That cross is the standard of him who conquered, not by fighting, but by dying; who came, not to destroy men's lives, but to save them. It is a standard, the very sight of which might teach you what sort of enemies you have to war against, if you are a christian, and how you may be sure to gain the victory.

I see you, while the standard of salvation is in

one hand, rushing on with a sword in the other, to the murder of your brother; and, under the banner of the cross, destroying the life of one who to the cross owes his salvation. Even from the holy sacrament itself, (for it is sometimes, at the same hour, administered in opposite camps) in which is signified the complete union of all christians, the warriors, who have just received it, run instantly to arms, and endeavour to plunge the dreadful steel into each other's vitals. Of a scene thus infernal, and fit only for the eyes of accursed spirits, who delight in mischief and misery, the pious warriors would make Christ the spectator, if it could be supposed that he would be present at it.

The absurdest circumstance of all those respecting the use of the cross as a standard is, that you see it glittering and waving high in air in both the contending armies at once. Divine service is also performed to the same Christ in both armies at the same time. What a shocking sight? Lo! crosses dashing against crosses, and Christ on this side firing bullets at Christ on the other; cross against cross, and Christ against Christ. The banner of the cross, significant of the christian profession, is used on each side, to strike terror into the opposite enemy. How dare they, on this occasion, to attack what, on all others, they adore? Because they are unworthy to bear the true cross at all, and rather deserve to be themselves crucified.

Let us now imagine we hear a soldier, among these fighting christians, saying the Lord's prayer. "Our Father," says he; O hardened wretch! can

you call him father, when you are just going to
cut your brother's throat? "Hallowed be thy
name:" how can the name of God be more impi-
ously unhallowed, than by mutual bloody murder
among you, his sons? "Thy kingdom come:" do
you pray for the coming of his kingdom, while
you are endeavouring to establish an earthly despotism, by spilling the blood of God's sons and
subjects? "Thy will be done on earth as it is in
heaven:" his will in heaven, is for peace, but you
are now meditating war. Dare you to say to your
Father in heaven "Give us this day our daily
bread;" when you are going, the next minute perhaps, to burn up your brother's corn-fields; and
had rather lose the benefit of them yourself, than
suffer him to enjoy them unmolested? With what
face can you say, "Forgive us our trespasses as
we forgive them that trespass against us," when,
so far from forgiving your own brother, you are
going, with all the haste you can, to murder him
in cold blood, for an alleged trespass that, after
all, is but imaginary. Do you presume to depre-
cate the danger of temptation, who, not without
great danger to yourself, are doing all you can
to force your brother into danger? Do you deserve to be delivered from evil, that is, from the
evil being, to whose impulse you submit yourself,
and by whose spirit you are now guided, in con-
triving the greatest possible evil to your brother?

Plato somewhere says, that when grecians war
with grecians, (notwithstanding they were separate and independent dynasties) it is not a war,
but an insurrection. He would not consider them
as a separate people, because they were united in

name and by vicinity. And yet the christians will
call it a war, and a just and necessary war too,
which, on the most trifling occasion, with such
soldiery and such weapons, one people professing
christianity, wages war with another people hold-
ing exactly the same creed, and professing the
same christianity.

The laws of some heathen nations ordained,
that he who should stain his sword with a brother's
blood, should be sewed up in a sack, and thrown
into the common sewer. Now they are no less
strongly united as brothers whom Christ has frat-
ernized, than those who are related by consanguinity. And yet, in war, there is a reward instead of
punishment for murdering a brother. Wretched
is the alternative forced upon us by war. He who
conquers is a murderer of his brother; and he
who is conquered, dies equally guilty of fratri-
cide, because he did his best to commit it.

After all this unchristian cruelty, and all this
inconsistency, the christian warriors execrate the
Turks as a tribe of unbelievers, strangers to Christ;
just as if, while they act in this manner, they
were christians themselves; or as if there could
be a more agreeable sight to the turks than to behold the christians running each other through
the body with the bayonet. The turks, say the
christians, sacrifice to the devil; but, as there can
be no victim so acceptable to the devil as a christian sacrificed by a christian, are not you, my good
christian, sacrificing to the devil as much as the
turk? Indeed, the evil one has in this case the
pleasure of two victims at a time, since he who
sacrifices is no less his victim than he who is sacri-

ficed by the hand of a christian and the sword of war. If any one favours the turks, and wishes to be on good terms with the devil, let him offer up such victims as these.

But I am well aware of the excuse which men, ever ingenious in devising mischief to themselves as well as others, offer in extenuation of their conduct in going to war. They allege, that they are compelled to it; that they are dragged against their will to war. I answer them, deal fairly; pull off the mask; throw away all false colours; consult your own heart, and you will find that anger, ambition, and folly are the compulsory force that has dragged you to war, and not any necessity; unless indeed you call the insatiable cravings of a covetous mind, necessity.

Reserve your outside pretences to deceive the thoughtless vulgar. God is not mocked with paint and varnish. Solemn days and forms of fasting, prayer, and thanksgiving, are appointed. Loud petitions are offered up to heaven for peace. The priests and the people roar out as vociferously as they can "give peace in our time, O Lord! We beseech thee to hear us, O Lord." Might not the Lord very justly answer and say, "why mock ye me, ye hypocrites? You fast and pray that I would avert a calamity which you have brought upon your own heads. You are deprecating an evil, of which yourselves are the authors."

Now, if every possible offence, every little occurrence not exactly to one's mind, is to excite a war, what is there in human affairs that will not furnish an occasion of deadly strife? In the tenderest connections of domestic life, and between the most affectionate husbands and wives, there is always some fault to be connived at, some omission or commission to be mutually forgiven, some occasion for reciprocal forbearance; unless you assert that it would be better to cut asunder, on the first dispute, all ties of affection.

Suppose some differences, like those of conjugal life, to happen between neighbouring princes, why should they immediately draw the sword, and proceed to the last sad extremities? There are laws, there are sagacious men, there are worthy clergymen, there are right reverend bishops, by whose salutary advice all disagreements might be reconciled, and all disturbance checked at its origin. Why do kings not make these, instead of the sword, their umpires? Even if the arbitrators were unjust, which is not likely, when removed from all undue influence, the disagreeing parties would come off with less injury than if they had recourse to arms; to the irrational and doubtful decision of war.

There is scarcely any peace so unjust, but it is preferable, upon the whole, to the justest war. Sit down, before you draw the sword, weigh every article, omit none, and compute the expence of blood as well as treasure which war requires, and the evils which it of necessity brings with it; and then see at the bottom of the account whether, after the greatest success, there is likely to be a balance in your favour.

The authority of the Roman pontiff is allowed to be paramount and decisive. Kings themselves allow it. And yet when nations, when kings are violently engaged in the most unnatural wars for years together, where is then the paramount and decisive authority of the pontiff, where then the power said to be second to none but Christ in heaven? On this occasion, if on any, this high power would be exerted, if the high pontiffs themselves were not slaves themselves to the same vile passions as the wretched kings and deluded people. The pontiff summons to war. He is obeyed. He summons to peace; why is he not obeyed as readily? If men, as they profess, really do prefer peace, and are reluctantly dragged to war, why do they obey pope Julius with so much alacrity when he calls them to war, and yield no obedience to pope Leo, when he invites them to concord and peace? If the authority of the Roman pontiff be really divine, surely it ought then to avail most when it prescribes that conduct which Christ taught as the only proper conduct. It is fair to conclude, that those whom Julius has authority enough to excite to a most destructive war, and whom Leo, a really religious pontiff,[1] cannot allure, by the most cogent arguments, to christian love and charity, are serving (I express myself tenderly of them) under the cloke of serving the church, nothing else but their own vile and selfish passions.

If you are in your heart weary of war, I will tell you how you may avoid it, and preserve a cordial and general amity.

Firm and permanent peace is not to be secured by marrying one royal family to another, nor by treaties and alliances made between such deceitful and imperfect creatures as men; for, from these

[1] Erasmus was mistaken in Leo's character.

very family connections, treaties, and alliances, we see wars chiefly originate. No; the fountains from which the streams of this evil flow, must be cleansed. It is from the corrupt passions of the human heart that the tumults of war arise. While each king obeys the impulse of his passions, the commonwealth, the community, suffers; and at the same time, the poor slave to his passions is frustrated in his private and selfish purposes.

Let kings then grow wise; wise for the people, not for themselves only; and let them be truly wise, in the proper sense of the word, not merely cunning, but really wise; so as to place their majesty, their felicity, their wealth, and their splendor in such things, and such only, as render them personally great, personally superior to those whom the fortune of birth has ranked, in a civil sense, below them. Let them acquire those amiable dispositions towards the commonwealth, the great body of the people, which a father feels for his family. Let a king think himself great in proportion as his people are good; let him estimate his own happiness by the happiness of those whom he governs; let him deem himself glorious in proportion as his subjects are free; rich, if the public are rich; and flourishing, if he can but keep the community flourishing, in consequence of uninterrupted peace.

Such should be our king, if we wish to establish a firm and lasting peace; and let the noblemen and magistrates imitate the king, rendered by these means worthy of imitation. Let the public good be the rule of their conduct; and so will they ultimately promote most effectually even their own private advantage.

Now, will a king of such a disposition as I have described, be easily prevailed upon to extort money from his own people to put it into the pockets of foreign mercenaries and alien subsidiaries? Will he reduce his own people to distress, perhaps even for bread, in order to fill the coffers of military despots and commanders? Will he be lavish of blood, as well as treasure, (neither of them his own) and expose the lives, as well as expend the property, of his people? No. I think he will know better.

Let him exercise his power as far as he pleases, within those bounds which he will always see clearly, when he remembers that he is a man governing men, a free man at the head of free men, a christian presiding over a nation of christians. In return for his good behaviour, let the people pay him just so much reverence, and yield him just so many privileges and prerogatives as for the public good, and no more. A good king will require no more; and as to the unreasonable desires of a bad king, the people should unite to check and repel them. Let there be on both sides a due regard paid to private happiness. Let the greatest share of honour be ever paid, not to warlike kings, (the world has sorely suffered for its folly in giving them glory) but to kings who entirely reject the war system, and by their understanding and counsels, not by force and arms, restore to bleeding human nature the blessings of concord and repose. Let him be called a great king, not who is continually augmenting his army, and providing military stores and engines of destruction, but who exerts every effort of his mind, and uses every advantage of his situation, to render armies, stores, and engines of destruction totally unnecessary. Truly glorious as is such an attempt; not one, in the long catalogue of kings and princes that has "strutted and fretted his hour upon the stage," every conceived the thought in his heart, except the emperor Dioclesian.

But if, after all, it is not possible that a war should be avoided, let it be so conducted, that the severest of its calamities may fall upon the heads of those who gave the occasion. Yet kings, instead of suffering at all by it, wage war in perfect consistency with their personal safety. The great men grow rich upon it. The largest part of the evil falls upon landholders, husbandmen, tradesmen, manufacturers, whom, perhaps the war does not in the least concern, and who never furnished the slightest cause for a national rupture.

In what consists the wisdom of a king, if he does not take these things into consideration? In what consists the gracious goodness, the tender feeling of a king, if he thinks such things beneath his notice?

Some method should be discovered to keep kings from shifting their thrones and dominions, and going from one dynasty to another, because innovations in matters of this kind always create disturbance, and disturbance produces war. This may easily be managed, if the children of kings are provided for, or established somewhere within their father's own dominions; or if it should appear expedient to connect them with neighbour-

ing crowned heads, let all hope of succession be
entirely cut off at the time when a marriage, or
any other mode of connection with foreign courts,
is negotiated. Nor let any king be allowed to sell
or alienate in any manner the least portion of his
dominions, as if free states were his private property. I say free states, for all states are free that
have kings, properly so called, to govern them.
States that are not free, are not under kings, whatever they may be called, but despots. By the inter-
marriage of kings and their progeny, and the
rights of succession which thence arise, a man
born in the bogs of Ireland may come to reign in
the East Indies; and another who was a king in
Syria, may all of a sudden start up an Italian
prince. Thus it may happen that neither country
shall have a king, while he abandons his former
dominions, and is not acknowledged by his newly
acquired ones; being a perfect stranger, born in
another world, for any thing they know to the
contrary. And in the mean time, while he is re-
ducing, subduing and exhausting part of his dominions, he is impoverishing and exhausting the
other. He sometimes loses both, while he is endeavouring to grasp both, and most likely is not
fit to govern either. Let kings once settle among
themselves, how much and how far each ought to
govern, and then let no marriage connection among
them either extend or contract; let no treaty alter
the limits once ascertained. Thus every one will
endeavour to improve his allotted portion to the
utmost of his power. All his efforts will be con-
centrated on one country, and he will endeavour
to transmit it to his posterity in a rich and flour-

ishing condition. The result will be, that when every one minds his own, all will thrive. Therefore let kings be attached to each other, not by political intermarriages, artificial and factitious ties, but by pure and sincere friendship; and above all, by a zeal similar and common to the whole tribe to promote the solid, substantial happiness of human nature. And let the king's successor be either he who is most nearly related to him, or he who shall be judged fittest for the momentous office, by the suffrages of the people. Let the other great men rest satisfied with being numbered among the honourable nobility. It is the duty of a king to enter into no party cabals, to know nothing of private passions or partialities, but to esteem all men and measures solely as they have a reference and tendency to the good of the public. Moreover, let the king avoid . travelling into foreign countries, let him never wish to pass the boundaries of his own dominions; but let him shew that he approves a proverbial saying, sanctioned by the wisdom of ages, *frons occipitio prior est:*[1] by which was intimated, that nothing goes

---

[1] Erasmus, whose good sense led him to delight in proverbs, thus explains his proverb in his Adagio. "Priscis agricolis celebratum adagium; quo significavit antiquitas rectius geri negotium, ubi praesens hae testes adest is cujus agitur negotium." The English proverb corresponding with it is rather too familiar for the occasion. The Latin may be thus translated: "The foreside sees more than the backside." Cato and Pliny use the proverb.

"Id nulli magis obferandum quam principi; si modo principis animum gerat, non praedonis, hoc est si publicum negotium cordi habet. At hodie fere episcopi et reges omnia alienis manibus, alienis auribus atque oculis agunt, neque quicquam minus ad se pertinere putant quam rempublicam, aut privatis suisque distenti, aut volupta-

on well when conducted by secondaries and mercenaries only, and in the absence of the principal.

Let him be persuaded that the best method of enriching and improving his realm, is not by taking from the territory of others, but by meliorating the condition of his own. When the expediency of war is discussed, let him not listen to the counsels of young ministers, who are pleased with the false glory of war, without considering its calamities, of which, from their age, it is impossible that they should have had personal experience. Neither let him consult those who have an interest in disturbing the public tranquillity and who are fed and fattened by the sufferings of the people. Let him take the advice of old men, whose integrity has been long tried, and who have shewn that they have an unfeigned attachment to their country. Nor let him, to gratify the passions or sinister views of one or two violent or artful men, rashly enter on a war; for war, once engaged in, cannot be put an end to at discretion. A measure the most dangerous to the existence of a state as a war must be, should not be entered into by a king, by a minister, by a junto of ambitious avaricious, or revengeful men, but by the full and unanimous consent of the whole people.

tibus occupati." This proverb deserves to be regarded by nobody more than a king; if he has the dispositions of a king, and not of a public plunderer, that is, if he has the public interest at heart. But now-a-days, bishops and kings transact all the proper business of their functions by other people's hands, ears, and eyes; nor do they think themselves concerned in any thing less, than in the care of the public good, being entirely occupied with pursuing their own private and selfish ends, or engaged in the pleasures of fashionable life and company.—*Erasmus.*

The causes of war are to be cut up, root and branch, on their first and slightest appearance. Many real injuries and insults must be connived at. Men must not be too zealous about a phantom called national glory; often inconsistent with individual happiness. Gentle behaviour on one side, will tend to secure it on the other; but the insolence of a haughty minister may give unpardonable offence, and be dearly paid for by the sufferings of the nation over which he domineers.

There are occasions when, if peace can be had in no other way, it must be purchased. It can scarcely be purchased too dearly, if you take into the account how much treasure you must inevitably expend in war; and what is of infinitely greater consequence than treasure, how many of the people's lives you save by peace. Though the cost be great, yet war would certainly cost you more; besides, (what is above all price) the blood of men, the blood of your own fellow-citizens and subjects, whose lives you are bound, by every tie of duty, to preserve, instead of lavishing away in prosecuting schemes of false policy, and cruel, selfish, villainous ambition. Only form a fair estimate of the quantity of mischief and misery of every kind and degree which you escape, and the sum of happiness you preserve in all the walks of private life, among all the tender relations of parents, husbands, children, among those whose poverty alone makes them soldiers, the wretched instruments of involuntary bloodshed; form but this estimate, and you will never repent the highest price you can pay for peace.

While the king does his duty as the guardian

and preserver, instead of the destroyer, of the people committed to his charge, let the right revverend the bishops do their duty likewise. Let the priests be priests indeed; preachers of peace and goodwill, and not the instigators of war, for the sake of pleasing a corrupt minister, in whose hands are livings, stalls, and mitres; let the whole body of the clergy remember the truly evangelical duties of their profession, and let the grave professors of theology in our universities, or wherever else they teach divinity, remember to teach nothing as men-pleasers unworthy of Christ. Let all the clergy, however they may differ in rank, order, sect, or persuasion, unite to cry down war, and discountenance it through the nation, by zealously and faithfully arraigning it from the pulpit. In the public functions of their several churches, in their private conversation and intercourse with the laity, let them be constantly employed in the christian, benevolent, humane work of **preaching,** recommending, and inculcating, peace. If, after all their efforts, the clergy cannot prevent the breaking out of war, let them never give it the slightest approbation, directly or indirectly, let them never give countenance to it by their presence at its silly parade or bloody proceedings, let them never pay the smallest respect to any great patron or prime minister, or courtier, who is the author or adviser of a state of affairs so contrary to their holy profession, and to every duty and principle of the christian religion, as is a state of war.

Let the clergy agree to refuse burial in consecrated ground to all who are slain in battle.[1] If there be any good men among the slain, and certainly there are very few, they will not lose the reward of christians in heaven, because they had not what is called christian burial. But the worthless, of whom the majority of warriors consists, will have one cause of that silly vanity and self-liking which attends and recommends their profession more than any thing else, entirely removed, when sepulchral honours are denied, after all the glory of being knocked on the head in battle, in the noble endeavour to kill a fellow-creature.

I am speaking all along of those wars which christians wage with christians, on trifling and unjustifiable occasions. I think very differently of wars, *bona fide,* just and necessary, such as are, in a strict sense of those words, purely defensive, such as with an honest and affectionate zeal for the country, repel the violence of invaders, and, at the hazard of life, preserve the public tranquillity.

But in the present state of things, the clergy (for of their conduct I proceed to speak) so far from acting as servants of Christ, in the manner I have recommended, do not hesitate to hang up flags, standards, banners, and other trophies of war, brought from the field of carnage, as ornaments of churches and great cathedrals. These trophies shall be all stained and smeared with the blood of men, for whom Christ shed his most precious blood, and shall be hung in the aisles of

[1] The words of Erasmus are "Satis sit in bello caesis, in profano sepulchrum dare." Here he goes too far; but it is in his benevolent design to prevent any being slain in battle in future.

the churches, among the tombs and images of apostles and martyrs, as if in future it were to be reckoned a mark of sanctity not to suffer martyrdom, but to inflict it; not to lay down one's life for the truth, but to take away the life of others for worldly purposes of vanity and avarice. It would be quite sufficient if the bloody rags were hung up in some corner of the Exchange or kept, as curiosities in a chest or closet, out of sight; disgraceful monuments they are of human depravity. The church, which ought to be kept perfectly pure, and emblematic of the purest of religions, should not be defiled with any thing stained with the blood of man, shed by the hand of man alienated, as is clear by the very act, both from Christ and from nature.

But you argue in defence of this indecent practice of hanging up flags or colours, as they are called, in churches, that the ancients used to deposit the monuments of their victories in the temples of their gods. It is true, but what were their gods but demons, delighting in blood and impurity? not the God, who is of purer eyes than to behold iniquity. Never let priests, dedicated to a God like this, have any thing to do with war, unless it is to put an end to it, and promote love and reconciliation. If the clergy were but unanimous in such sentiments, if they would inculcate them every where, there is no doubt, notwithstanding the great power of the secular arm, that their authority, personal and professional, would have a preponderance, against the influence of courts and ministers of state, and thus prevent war, the calamity of human nature.

But if there is a fatal propensity in the human heart to war, if the dreadful disease is interwoven with the constitution of man, so that it cannot abstain from war, why is not vent given to the virulence in exertions against the common enemy of christianity, the unbelieving Turk? Yet—even here let me pause—is not the Turk a man—a brother? Then it were far better to allure him by gentle, kind, and friendly treatment, by exhibiting the beauty of our christian religion in the innocence of our lives, than by attacking him with the drawn sword, as if he were a savage brute, without a heart to feel, or a reasoning faculty to be persuaded. Nevertheless, if we must of necessity go to war, as I said before, it is certainly a less evil to contend with an infidel, than that christians should mutually harass and destroy their own fraternity. If charity will not cement their hearts, certainly one common enemy may unite their hands, and though this may not be a cordial unity, yet it will be better than a real rupture.

Upon the whole it must be said, that the first and most important step towards peace, is sincerely to desire it. They who once love peace in their hearts, will eagerly seize every opportunity of establishing or recovering it. All obstacles to it they will despise or remove, all hardships and difficulties they will bear with patience, so long as they keep this one great blessing (including as it does so many others) whole and entire. On the contrary, men, in our times, go out of their way to seek occasions of war; and whatever makes for peace, they run down in their sophistical speeches, or even basely conceal from the public;

but whatever tends to promote their favourite war system, they industriously exaggerate and inflame, not scrupling to propagate lies of the most mischievous kind, false or garbled intelligence, and the grossest misrepresentation of the enemy. I am ashamed to relate what real and dreadful tragedies in real life, they found on these vile despicable trifles, from how small an ember they blow up a flame and set the world on fire. Then they summon before them the whole catalogue of supposed injuries received, and each party views its own grievance with a glass that magnifies beyond all bounds; but as for benefits received, they all fall into the profoundest oblivion as soon as received; so that upon the whole, an impartial observer would swear that great men love war for its own sake, with their hearts and souls, provided their own persons are safe.

After all the pretences thrown out, and the artifices used, to irritate the vulgar, there often lurks (as the true cause of wars) in the bosom of kings, some private, mean, and selfish motive, which is to force their subjects to take up weapons to kill one another, at the word of command, and as they wish to evince their loyalty. But, instead of a private and selfish object, there ought to be an object, in which not only the public, that is, not only one single community, but in which man, human nature, is deeply interested to justify the voluntary commencement of a war.

But when kings can find no cause of this kind, as indeed they seldom can, then they set their wits to work to invent some fictitious but plausible occasion for a rupture. They will make use of the names of foreign countries, artfully rendered odious to the people, in order to feed the popular odium, till it becomes ripe for war, and thirsts for the blood of the outlandish nation, whose very name is rendered a cause of hostility. This weakness and folly of the very lowest classes of the people, the grandees increase by artful insinuations, watchwords, and nicknames, cunningly thrown out in debates, pamphlets, and journals. Certain of the clergy, whose interest it is to cooperate with the grandees in any unchristian work, join, with great effect, aided by religion, in a pious imposition on the poor. Thus, for instance, an Englishman they say, is the natural enemy of a Frenchman, because he is a Frenchman. A man born on this side the river Tweed must hate a Scotchman, because he is a Scotchman. A German naturally disagrees with a Frank, a Spaniard with both. O villainous depravity! The name of a place or region, in itself a circumstance of indifference, shall be enough to dissever your hearts more widely than the distance of place, your persons! A name is nothing, but there are many circumstances, very important realities, which ought to endear and unite men of different nations. As an Englishman, you bear ill-will to a Frenchman. Why not rather, as a man to a man, do you not bear him good-will? Why not as a christian to a christian? How happens it, that such a frivolous thing as a name avails more with you than the tender ties of nature, the strong bonds of christianity? Place, local distance, separates the persons of men, but not their minds. Hearts can gravitate to each other through intervening seas and mountains.

The river Rhine once separated the Frenchman from the German, but it was beyond its power to separate the christian from the christian. The Pyrenean mountains divide the Spaniards from the French, but they break not that invisible bond which holds them together in defiance of all partition, the communion of the church. A little gut of a sea divides the English from the French; but if the whole Atlantic ocean rolled between them, it could not disjoin them as men united by nature; and, while they mutually retain the christian religion, still more indissolubly cemented by grace.

The Apostle Paul expresses his indignation, that christians, separating into sects, should say, "I am of Apollos; I am of Cephas; I am of Paul:" nor would he suffer the unnatural distinction of a name to parcel out Christ, who is one with all his members, and who has formed all into one inviolable whole. And shall we think the common name of a native country cause sufficient why one race of men should hunt down another race of men, even to extermination; should engage them with each other in a *bellum ad internecionem*; a war, to cut off, on one side or the other, man, woman and child,. and leave not a tongue to tell the tale?

The hostile distinction of different nations as natural enemies, because they are separated by place, and diversified by name, is not enough to satisfy some among the blood-thirsty wretches who delight in war. Such is the depravity of their minds, that they seek occasions of difference where none is afforded either by nature or institution.

They would divide France against itself, in verbal and nominal distinctions of the inhabitants; a country which is not divided by seas, or by mountains, and is indeed one and indivisible, however artful men may endeavour to cause divisions in it by distinctions merely nominal. Thus some of the French they will denominate Germans, lest the circumstance of identity of name should produce that unanimity which they diabolically wish to interrupt.

Now, if, in courts of judicature, the judge will not admit of suits which are frivolous and vexatious; if he will not admit of all sorts of evidence, especially that which arises from a personal pique and resentment, how happens it that, in a business of far more consequence to human nature even than courts of judicature, in an affair the most odious and abominable, such as the promoting discord among human creatures and whole neighbouring nations, causes the most frivolous and vexatious are freely admitted as competent and valid. Let the lovers of discord, and the promoters of bloodshed between nations, divided only by a name and a channel, rather reflect, that this world, the whole of the planet called earth, is the common country of all who live and breathe upon it, if the title of one's country is allowed to be a sufficient reason for unity among fellow-countrymen; and let them also remember, that all men, however distinguished by political or accidental causes, are sprung from the same parents, if consanguinity and affinity are allowed to be available to concord and peace. If the church also is a sub-division of this one great universal family, a family of itself consisting of all who belong to that church, and if the being of the same family necessarily connects all the members in a common interest and a common regard for each other, then the opposers must be ingenious in their malice, if they can deny, that all who are of the same church, the grand catholic church of all christendom, must also have a common interest, a common regard for each other, and therefore be united in love.

In private life, you bear with some things in a brother-in-law which you bear with only because he is a brother-in-law; and will you bear with nothing in him who by the tie of the same religion is also a brother? You pardon many little offences on account of nearness of kindred, and will you pardon nothing on account of an affinity founded in religion? Yet, there is no doubt but that the closest possible tie among all the christian brotherhood, is confraternity in Christ.

Why are you always fixing your attention upon the sore place, where the insult of injury received from a fellow-creature festers and rankles? If you seek peace and ensue it, as you ought to do, you will rather say to yourself, "he hurt me in this instance, it is true; but in other instances he has often served or gratified me, and in this one he was perhaps incited to momentary wrong by passion, mistake, or by another's impulse." As, in the poet Homer, the persons who seek to effect a reconciliation between Agamemnon and Achilles, throw all the blame of their quarrel on the Goddess Atè; so in real life, offences that cannot be excused consistently with strict veracity, should, good-naturedly, be imputed to ill-fortune,

or, if you please, to a man's evil-genius; that the
resentment may be transferred from men to those
imaginary beings, who can bear the load, however
great, without the slightest inconvenience.

Why should men shew more sagacity in creat-
ing misery, than in securing and increasing the
comforts of life? Why should they be more quick-
sighted in finding evil than good? All men of
sense weigh, consider, and use great circumspec-
tion, before they enter upon any private business
of momentous consequence. And yet they throw
themselves headlong into war, with their eyes
shut; notwithstanding war is that kind of evil
which, when once admitted, cannot be excluded
again at will; but usually, from a little one, becomes a very great one; from a single one, multiplies into a complication; from an unbloody con-
test, changes to carnage, and at last rises to a
storm, which does not overwhelm merely one or
two, and those the chief instigators to the mischief, but all the unoffending people also; con-
founding the innocent with the guilty.

If the poor people, of the very lowest order, are
too thoughtless to consider these things, it can be
no excuse for the king and the nobles, whose in-
dispensable duty it is to consider them well; and
it is the particular business of the clergy to enforce these pacific opinions with every argument
which ingenuity and learning can derive from
reason and religion; to enforce them, I say, and
inculcate them on the minds of both the great,
vulgar, and the small; "instantly, in season, and
out of season"; whether they "will bear, or
whether they will forbear." Something will at

last stick, if it is incessantly applied; and, therefore, let the pulpits and conversation of the clergy
teach the bland doctrines of peace and love every-
where and always.

Mortal man! (for so I address thee, even on a
throne) dost thou exult at hearing the rumour of
an ensuing war? Check thy joy for a moment,
and examine, accurately, the nature and consequences of peace, and the nature and consequences
of war; what blessings follow in the train of peace,
and what curses march in the rear of war; and
then form a true and solid judgment, whether it
can ever be expedient to exchange peace for war?
If it is a goodly and beautiful sight to behold a
country flourishing in the highest prosperity; its
cities well built, its lands well cultivated, the best
of laws well executed; arts, sciences, and learning,
those honourable employments of the human mind,
encouraged; men's morals virtuous and honest;
then may it please your Majesty to lay your hand
on your heart, and let your conscience whisper
to you, "All this happiness I must disturb or
destroy, if I engage in this meditated war." On
the other hand, if you ever beheld the ruin of
cities, villages burnt, churches battered down,
fields laid desolate, and, if the sight could wring
a tear of pity from thine eye, then, Sire, remember
that these are the blasted fruits of accursed war!
If you think it a great inconvenience to be obliged
to admit an inundation of hired soldiers into your
realms, to feed and clothe them at the expence of
your subjects, to be very submissive to them,
meanly to court their favour, in order to keep
them in good humour, well affected, and loyal;

and, after all, to trust (which is unavoidable in these circumstances) your own person and your safety to the discretion of such a rabble; recollect, that such is the condition of a state of warfare, and that these evils, great as they are, become necessary, when you have made yourself their slave, in order to enslave or destroy an imaginary enemy.

If you detest robbery and pillage, remember these are among the duties of war; and that, to learn how to commit them adroitly, is a part of military discipline. Do you shudder at the idea of murder? You cannot require to be told, that to commit it with dispatch, and by wholesale, constitutes the celebrated art of war. If murder were not learned by this art, how could a man, who would shudder to kill one individual, even when provoked, go, in cold blood, and cut the throats of many for a little paltry pay, and under no better authority than a commission from a mortal as weak, wicked and wretched as himself, who does not perhaps know even his person, and would not care if both his body and soul were annihilated? If there cannot be a greater misfortune to the commonwealth, than a general neglect and disobedience of the laws, let it be considered as a certain truth, that the voice of law, divine or human, is never heard amid the clangor of arms, and the din of battle. If you deem debauchery, rape, incest, and crimes of still greater turpitude than these, foul disgraces to human nature, depend upon it that war leads to all of them, in their most aggravated atrocity. If impiety, or a total neglect of religion, is the source of all villany, be assured that religion is always overwhelmed in the storms of war. If you think that the very worst possible condition of society, when the worst of men possess the greatest share of power, you may take it as an infallible observation, that the wickedest, most unprincipled, and most unfeeling wretches bear the greatest sway in a state of war; and that such as would come to the gallows in time of peace, are men of prime use and energy in the operations of a siege or a battle. For, who can lead the troops through secret ways more skilfully than an experienced robber, who has spent an apprenticeship to the art among thieves? Who will pull down a house, or rob a church, more dexterously than one who has been trained to burglary and sacrilege? Who will plunge his bayonet into the enemy's heart, or rip up his bowels with more facility of execution, than a practised assassin, or thorough-paced cut-throat by profession? Who is better qualified to set fire to a village, or a city, or a ship, than a notorious incendiary? Who will brave the hardships and perils of the sea better than a pirate long used to rob, sink, and destroy merchant vessels inoffensively traversing the great waters? In short, if you would form an adequate idea of the villany of war, only observe by whom it is carried into actual execution.

If nothing can be a more desirable object to a pious king, than the safety and welfare of those who are committed to his charge, then, consistently with this object, war must of necessity be held in the greatest conceivable abhorrence. If it is the happiness of a king to govern the happy, he cannot but delight in peace. If a good king wishes for nothing so much as to have his people good, like himself, he must detest war, as the foul sink of sin as well as misery. If he has sense and liberality enough to consider his subjects' riches, the best and truest opulence he can himself possess, then let him shun war by all possible means; because, though it should turn out ever so fortunate, it certainly diminishes every body's property, and expends that which was earned by honest, honourable, and useful employments, on certain savage butchers of the human race. Let him also consider again and again, that every man is apt to flatter himself that his own cause is a good one; that every man is pleased with his own schemes and purposes; and that every measure appears to a man agitated with passion the most equitable, though it is the most unjust, the most imprudent, and the most fallacious in the issue. But, suppose the cause the justest in the world, the event the most prosperous, yet take into the account all the damages of war, of every kind and degree, and weigh them in the balance with all the advantages of victory, and you will find the most brilliant success not worth the trouble.

Seldom can a conquest be gained without the effusion of blood. Therefore, in the midst of the rejoicings, illuminations, acclamations, and all the tumult of joy, excited by knaves among fools, it must occur to a king with a feeling heart that he has embrued hands, hitherto unspotted, in the pollution of human gore. Add to this circumstance, distressing to every humane heart, the injury done to the morals of the people, and the general good order and discipline of the state,

and you will find this a loss which neither money,
nor territory, nor glory, can compensate. You
have exhausted your treasury, you have fleeced
your people, you have loaded peaceable good subjects with unnecessary burdens, and you have
encouraged the wicked unprincipled adventurers
in acts of rapine and violence; and, after all, even
when the war is put an end to, the bad consequences of the war still remain, not to be removed
by the most splendid victory. The taste for sci-
ence, arts, and letters, languishes a long while.
Trade and commerce continue shackled and im-
peded. Though you should be able to block up
the enemy, yet, in doing it, you, in fact, block up
yourself and your own people; for neither you
nor they dare enter the neighbouring nation,
which, before the war, was open to egress and
regress; while peace, by opening an universal
intercourse among mankind, renders, in some
measure, all the neighbouring dynasties one common country.

Consider what mighty matters you have done
by thus boldly rushing into war. Your own hered-
itary dominions can scarcely be called your own.
The possession is rendered insecure, being constantly exposed to hostile invasion. In order to
demolish a poor little town, how much artillery,
how much camp-equipage, and all other military
apparatus, do you find requisite? You must build
a sort of temporary town, in order to overthrow
a real one; and, for less money than the whole
business of destruction costs you, you might build
another town by the side of that you are going to
level in the dust, where human beings might enjoy,

if you would let them, the comforts of that life
which God has been pleased to bestow in peace and
plenty. In order to prevent the enemy from going
out of the gates of his own town, you are obliged
to sleep for months out of yours in a tent of the
open air, and continue in a state of transportation
and exile from your own home. You might build
new walls for less than it costs you to batter down
the old ones with your cannon-balls, and all the
expensive contrivances formed for the hellish purposes of marring and demolishing the works of
human industry. In this cursory computation of
your expence, (for that I am chiefly considering,
and the gain that accrues from victory) I do not
reckon the vast sums that stick to the fingers of
commissioners, contractors, generals, admirals, and
captains, which is certainly a great part of the
whole.

If you could bring all these articles into a
fair and honest calculation, I will painfully suffer myself to be every where driven from you
mortals as I am, unless it should appear that you
might have purchased peace, without a drop of
blood, at a tenth part of the expenditure. But
you think it would be mean and humiliating, inconsistent with your own and your nation's honour, to put up with the slightest injury: now I
can assure you, that there is no stronger proof
of a poor spirit, a narrow, cowardly, and unkingly
heart, than revenge; especially as a king does not
risk his own person in taking it, but employs the
money of the people and the courage of the poor.
You think it inconsistent with your august majesty, and that it would be departing from your

royal dignity, to recede one inch from your strict right in favour of a neighbouring king, though related to you by consanguinity or marriage, and perhaps one who has formerly rendered you beneficial services. Poor strutting mortal! how much more effectually do you let down your august majesty and royal dignity when you are obliged to sacrifice with oblations of gold to foreign and barbarous mercenaries, to the lowest dregs, the most profligate wretches on the face of the earth; when, with the most abject adulation, and in the meanest form of a petitioner, you send ambassadors or commissioners to the vilest and most mischievous nations around, to ask them to receive your subsidies; trusting your august majesty's life, and the property and political existence of your people, to the good faith of allies, who appear to have no regard to the most sacred engagements, and are no less inclined to violate justice than humanity.

If the preservation of peace is attended with the necessity of submitting to some circumstances rather disadvantageous, and perhaps unjust, do not say to yourself, that you incur such a loss by resolving on peace instead of war, but that you purchase the inestimable benefit of peace at such a price. You could not get it cheaper; but the consolation is that it cannot be bought too dearly. Yet methinks a royal objector says, "I would very willingly give up such and such points if I were a private man, and the things in question were my own property; but I am a king, and, whether I like it or not, am under the necessity of acting, as I do, for the public."

For the public, says your majesty? Let me tell you, "that king will not easily be induced to enter on a war, who has no regard but for the public." On the contrary, we see that almost all the real causes of wars are things which have no reference at all to the welfare of the public. Is your object to claim and gain possession of this or that part of another's territory, what is that to the welfare of the people? Do you desire to take royal revenge on a crowned head in your vicinity, who has presumed to refuse your daughter in marriage, or repudiated her after marriage; what is that to the welfare of the people? How is it, in the smallest degree, a business of the state, the community at large? If you mean really to support your august majesty and royal dignity, the only way is, to support the character of a good, just, and wise man, by taking all these things into your most serious consideration, and acting accordingly.

Which of you modern kings ever extended his empire so widely, or governed with so much majesty and dignity, as Augustus Caesar? But he, in all his glory, was desirous of relinquishing his power, if the people could have found any prince to preside over them with more advantage to the commonwealth. The saying of a certain emperor of antiquity, is justly celebrated by the best writers; "perish, said he, my sons and heirs, if any other successor can be found more likely than any of them to consult the happiness of the people." These two emperors, not being christians, are called impious, heathenish men, by christians; by those who would go to war, in defence of law,

order, and religion; and yet such benevolent dispositions did these impious, heathen emperors display towards promoting the welfare of the people,
the happiness of man in society! In the mean-
time, christian emperors consider a whole christian people as a swinish multitude, as so little
worthy of their regard, that they would set the
world on fire, without consulting the people, to
revenge the disappointment of their own selfish
desires or to secure their full gratification.

Still I hear certain potentates captiously ex-
claiming, that it does not signify arguing, and that
they could not be personally safe if they did not
repel by fire and sword the power of ill-designing
men, who, not having the fear of God before their
eyes, might even attack, with success, their own
august majesty. How happens it, I ask them in
return, that among all the Roman emperors, Antonius Pius and Antonius the philosopher were
the only ones that were never attacked? From
these two instances it appears, that no kings sit
more firmly on their thrones, than they who shew
that they are ready at any time to quit them, when
their resignation appears likely to benefit the public; and that their power is a trust resumable at
will, reposed in them by the people for the good
of the people, and not to gratify their own pride
or avarice, by lavishing away other men's blood
and money.

May it please your most christian majesties! if
nothing will move you, if neither the feelings of
nature, the reflections of conscience, nor the actual
pressure of calamity; at least, let the reproach of
the christian profession (for which you pretend

to be so zealous) bring you back to long relinquished christian unanimity.

May it please you, who would go to war in defence of religion, as well as of law and order, to consider how small a portion of the terraqueous globe is occupied by christians. And this portion, small as it is, constitutes what is called in the scriptures, a city situated on a holy mountain, to be constantly reverenced, and preserved inviolate, both by God and man.

But what must we suppose a nation of atheists, (if any such there be) or of unbelievers in Christ, think and say? what reproaches must they vomit out against Christ, when they see his professed followers cutting one another in pieces, from more trifling causes than the heathens; with greater cruelty than atheists, and with more destructive instruments of mutual murder than pagans could ever find in their hearts to use, or in their understanding to contrive.

Whose invention was a cannon? Was it not the invention of the meek, lowly, merciful followers of Jesus Christ, whose law was love, and whose last legacy to his disciples and the world, peace? The cannon was the contrivance of christians; and to add to their infamy, it is usual to mark the names of the apostles and to engrave the images of saints upon the great guns. Cruel mockery of Christ, and of human misery! Paul, the constant teacher and preacher of peace, gives a name to a piece of artillery, and is thus made to hurl a deadly ball at the head of a christian; The church militant with a vengeance!

If we are so anxious, as we pretend, to support

religion, law, and order, and particularly to convert an unbelieving nation to christianity, let us
first prove ourselves to be sincere followers of
Christ. Will the nation to whom we intend the
favour of conversion to christianity by fire and
sword, believe that we ourselves are christians,
when they see, what is too evident to be denied,
that no people on earth quarrel and fight, one
among another, more savagely than we christians;
though Christ, the founder of the very religion
which we mean to propagate among them, declared
his utter detestation of all contention, and particularly of war?

A great heathen poet expresses his admiration,
that among heathens, whom we pity for their ignorance, though there is a time when men have
enough of the sweetest enjoyments of life, as of
sleep, of food, of wine, of the dance, and the mel-
ody of music, yet that they seem never to have
enough of the miseries of war. What he said of
the heathens, his contemporaries and countrymen,
is strictly true among those to whom the very
name of war, the very word, (as signifying a thing
disgraceful to human nature) ought to be held in
utter abomination.

Rome, ancient Rome, mad as she was with mar-
tial rage, and intoxicated with the vanity of military glory, yet sometimes shut the temple of her
Janus. How then happens it, that among you, ye
christian kings and people, no recess, no holiday,
no vacations, no rest is allowed in the work of
war? With what face should you dare to recom-
mend the christian religion to an unbelieving nation, as the religion of peace, when you yourselves

are never at peace, but engaged in bitter quarrels and hostilities among each other, without the least intermission? What encouragement must it give the common enemy to see you thus divided. Divide and conquer, is a maxim; and no victory is easier than that over men turn to pieces by internal dissension. Would you, as a nation of christians, be formidable to those who have renounced, or never knew, christianity? To be formidable, be united.

Why should you, wretched mortals, of your own accord, poison the pleasure, embitter all the enjoyment of this present life, and at the same time cut yourselves off from all chance of future felicity? Few and evil are the days of man, numberless the unavoidable calamities of human life; but a great part of the misery may be alleviated by love and friendship; while, by mutual kind offices all men afford each other, in difficulties that are surmountable, assistance, and, under distress that admits no remedy, consolation. The good that falls to man's lot will be sweeter in its enjoyment and more extensive in its effects, by concord; while every man considers every other man as a friend, imparts as a share of his possessions where he can; and, where he cannot, makes him a partaker of his good-humour and good-will.

How frivolous! what childish trifles! and how soon will they perish like yourselves! about which you make such disturbance; and, to obtain which, you deal death and desolation round the land. Death! you have no occasion for swords and muskets to accelerate it. Poor insects of a summer's day! death hovers over all of you, in act to strike, with unerring dart, the king in all his glory, at the head of his armies, as suddenly as the labourer in the field and the manufactory. What a tumult is excited by an animalcule, with a crown on his head! a being who will soon vanish, like the smoke into the air, and leave not a vestige of its existence. At the very portal of your palace, at the entrance of your military pavilion, lo! the brink of eternity! Why then will you fret and fume about shadows, phantoms, air-drawn objects of a waking dream, as if this life were endless, and there were time enough in it to be wantonly mad and miserable.

O wretched men! ye who will not believe in the future happiness of the good, or who dare not hope it for yourselves under that description. Most unreasonable, as well as miserable, if you think that the road to the blissful country of Heaven lies through the field of battle and the walks of war! The very bliss of Heaven itself is but an undescribable union of beatified minds; to take place when that shall be fully accomplished, which Christ earnestly prayed for to his heavenly Father, desiring that christians might be as intimately and mysteriously united to each other, as he is with the Father. How can you ever be fit for this perfect union, unless you meditate upon it in the interval, and endeavour with your utmost efforts to attain it? As the transition would be too sudden and violent, from a foul and filthy glutton to an angel of light; so would it be, from a bloody warrior to the company of martyrs, and those who have kept themselves unspotted from the world, unstained with human gore.

Enough, and more than enough, of christian blood, enough of human blood, has been already spilt; enough have you acted the part of madmen to your mutual destruction; enough have you sacrificed to the evil spirits of hell; long enough have you been acting a tragedy for the entertainment of unbelievers. I pray you, after so long and sad experience of the evils of war, (submitted to by the principal sufferers a great while ago too patiently) repent, and be wise.

Let the folly that is past be imputed, if you will, to the destinies, to any thing you please. Let the christians vote, what the heathens sometimes voted, an entire amnesty of all past errors and misfortunes; but, for the time to come, apply yourselves, one and all, to the preservation and perpetuation of peace. Bind up discord, not with hempen bands liable to be broken or untwisted, but with chains of steel and adamant, never to be burst asunder, till time shall be no more.

Kings! to you I make my first appeal. On your nod, such is the constitution of human affairs, the happiness of mortals is made to depend. You assume to be the images and representatives of Christ, your sovereign. Then, as you wish men to hear your voice shew the example of obedience, and hear the voice of your Sovereign Lord, commanding you, upon your duty, to seek peace and abolish war. Be persuaded that the world, wearied with its long continued calamities, demands this, and has a right to insist on your immediate compliance.

Priests! to you I appeal as consecrated to the God of Love and Mercy. On your conscience I require you to promote, with all the zeal of your hearts and abilities of your minds, that which you know is most agreeable to God; and to explode, discountenance, and repel, with equal ardour and activity, what you know in your hearts he abhors.

Preachers of all denominations! to you I appeal. Preach the gospel of peace. Let the doctrines of peace and good-will for ever resound in the ears of the people.

Bishops, and all who are pre-eminent in ecclesiastical dignity! I call upon you, that the high authority and influence which you possess over the minds of both kings and people, may be exerted to bind upon their hearts, with bonds indissoluble, the sacred obligations to peace.

Dukes, lords, grandees, placemen, and magistrates, of every description! I appeal to you, that your hearty good-will may co-operate in the work of peace, with the wisdom of kings, and the piety of priests.

I appeal to all who call themselves christians! I urge them, as they would manifest their sincerity, and preserve their consistency, to unite with one heart and one soul, in the abolition of war, and the establishment of perpetual and universal peace.

Here, and in this instance, shew the world, how much can be effected by the union of the multitude, the mass of the people, against the despotism of the few and the powerful.

Hither let all ranks and orders, equally zealous and intent in the glorious cause, bring and unite all their wisdom and abilities. Let eternal concord connect those whom Nature has connected

in many points, and Christ in all. Let all act with
equal zeal in accomplishing a purpose which will
contribute equally to the happiness of all. Hither
every circumstance invites you to co-operate; in the
first place, the natural feelings of man's heart, the
spontaneous dictates of common humanity; and,
in the next, the author and disposer of all human
happiness, Christ. The innumerable blessings of
peace, and the unutterable miseries of war, I have
already endeavoured to describe. Hither also the
inclinations of kings themselves, in our times,
(the favourable influence of God's grace impelling
their minds to concord) seem to invite. Behold!
the mild and pacific[1] Leo, acting the part of
Christ's true vicar, has lifted up the signal of
peace, and exhorted all men to flock to its standard. If then you are true sheep, follow your
shepherd. If you are true sons, listen to the voice
of your Father. Hither likewise Francis, king of
France and the most christian king, not in title
only, summons you. He disdains not to purchase
peace; nor does he regard his own pomp and external dignity, so long as he can promote and preserve the public tranquillity. He has shewn that
the true splendor of royalty, the real majesty of
a king, consists in an endeavour to deserve well
of the human race, to promote the happiness of
individuals, and not to involve them in misery and
destruction, in a wild quixotic pursuit of glory.
Hither also you are called by the renowned Charles

[1] Erasmus was much mistaken in Leo and other potentates of his time. But it was necessary, for personal
safety, to pay such compliments. Besides, that praise
which they did not deserve was a severe reproach, and
might stimulate them to endeavour to deserve it.

the fifth, a young man of a disposition naturally good, and happily not yet corrupted. Caesar Maximilian appears to have no objection to peace, nor does Henry, the famous king of England, refuse his concurrence.

As to the people; in all these countries the greater part of the people certainly detest war, and most devoutly wish for peace. A very few of them, indeed, whose unnatural happiness depends upon the public misery, may wish for war; but be it yours to decide, whether it is equitable or not, that the unprincipled selfishness of such wretches should have more weight than the anxious wishes of all good men united. You plainly see, that hitherto nothing has been effectually done towards permanent peace by treaties, no good end answered by royal intermarriages, neither by violence, nor by revenge. Now then it is time to pursue different measures; to try the experiment, what a placable disposition, and a mutual desire to do acts of friendship and kindness, can accomplish in promoting national amity. It is the nature of wars, that one should sow the seeds of another; it is the nature of revenge to produce reciprocal revenge. Now then, on the contrary, let kindness generate kindness, one good turn become productive of another; and let him be considered as the most kingly character, the greatest and best potentate, who is ready to concede the most from his own strict right, and to sacrifice all exclusive privilege to the happiness of the people.

What has been done by mere human policy, and for temporal purposes only, has not yet succeeded; but Christ will give success to those pious designs, which shall appear to be undertaken under his auspices and by his authority. He will be present and propitious, and favour those who favour that state of human affairs, which he himself evidently appeared, while on earth, so remarkably, decidedly to promote.

Let the public good overcome all private and selfish regards of every kind and degree; though in truth, even private and selfish regards, and every man's own interest, will be best promoted by the preservation of peace. Kings will find, that to reign is a more glorious thing than ever it has been, when they reign by the mild authority of law, and not by arms and violence. The nobility will find their dignity greater in itself, and established on more reasonable, and therefore more permanent principles. The clergy will enjoy their ease with less interruption. The people will possess tranquillity with greater plenty, and plenty with greater tranquillity, than they yet have ever known. The christian profession will become respectable to the enemies of the cross. Finally, every man will become dear and pleasing to every other man; all will be beloved by all! and, what is still more desirable, beloved also by Christ; to become acceptable to whom is the highest felicity of human nature.

FINIS.